W9-BRU-010

GLOBAL GUARDIANS

SOLVING THE ENERGY CRISIS

Dwayne Hicks

PowerKiDS
press

New York

Published in 2017 by The Rosen Publishing Group, Inc.
29 East 21st Street, New York, NY 10010

First Edition

Editor: Theresa Morlock
Book Design: Reann Nye

Photo Credits: Cover (background), pp. 1–24 (background) jwblinn/
Shutterstock.com; cover (map), pp.1–24 Buslik/Shutterstock.com; cover (top),
p. 1 pedrosala/Shutterstock.com; cover (bottom) manfredxy/Shutterstock.com;
p. 4 f-f-f-f/Shutterstock.com; p. 5 abutyrin/Shutterstock.com; p. 7 (natural gas)
Chepko Danil Vitalevich/Shutterstock.com; p. 7 (coal) xtrekx/Shutterstock.com;
p. 7 (oil) hiroshi teshigawara/Shutterstock.com; p. 8 Rena Schild/Shutterstock.com;
p. 9 arindambanerjee/Shutterstock.com; p. 11 Viktorus/Shutterstock.com;
p. 13 Hero Images/Getty Images; p. 14 Stocktrek Images/Getty Images;
p. 15 esbobeldijk/Shutterstock.com; p. 17 Steve Meese/Shutterstock.com;
p. 18 Bryan Busovicki/Shutterstock.com; p. 19 Tupungato/Shutterstock.com;
p. 20 Cardaf/Shutterstock.com; p. 21 r.classen/Shutterstock.com;
p. 22 Alistair Berg/DigitalVision/Getty Images.

Library of Congress Cataloging-in-Publication Data

Names: Hicks, Dwayne, author.
Title: Solving the energy crisis / Dwayne Hicks.
Description: New York : PowerKids Press, [2017] | Series: Global guardians |
   Includes bibliographical references and index.
Identifiers: LCCN 2016037024| ISBN 9781508152781 (6 pack) | ISBN
   9781499428735 (library bound book) | ISBN 9781499427523 (pbk. book)
Subjects: LCSH: Renewable energy sources–Juvenile literature.
Classification: LCC TJ808.2 .H53 2017 | DDC 333.79–dc23
LC record available at https://lccn.loc.gov/2016037024

Manufactured in China

CPSIA Compliance Information: Batch #BW17PK: For Further Information contact Rosen Publishing, New York, New York at 1-800-237-9932

CONTENTS

POWER UP!. 4

FINDING OUT ABOUT
FOSSIL FUELS. 6

NONRENEWABLE RESOURCES 8

GETTING HOTTER 10

CONSERVATION IS KEY. 12

SAVING ENERGY WITH THE SUN . .14

POWERFUL WIND ENERGY 16

WATER WORKS. 18

SPLITTING APART. 20

MAKING A DIFFERENCE 22

GLOSSARY. 23

INDEX 24

WEBSITES. 24

POWER UP!

People depend on energy every day. It runs our computers, washing machines, and TVs. Energy powers our cars so we can get from place to place. Energy heats and cools our homes and gives us light when it's dark.

Most of the energy used in the United States comes from burning **fossil fuels**. However, scientists are worried we're using too much too quickly, and that means we could run out. This shortage is called an **energy crisis**. What caused the energy crisis?

batteries

4

coal

Energy is the ability to do work. It comes from a physical source, such as coal, or a chemical source, such as the matter inside batteries. We use both in our everyday lives.

FINDING OUT ABOUT FOSSIL FUELS

There are three kinds of fossil fuels—oil, coal, and natural gas. Oil is a thick, dark liquid. Coal is a type of black rock. Oil and coal formed from animals and plants millions of years ago. Natural gas is a colorless gas that has no smell.

Each fossil fuel is used for different purposes. Cars run on gasoline, which is made from oil. Natural gas is used to heat buildings. It's often used in stoves to cook food. Oil and coal are burned in power plants to make some of the electricity we use.

CONSERVATION CLUES

About 40 percent of the electricity in the United States is made by coal.

natural gas

coal

oil

The processes used to remove fossil fuels from the earth can be very **destructive**. Mining for coal and drilling for oil pollutes land and sources of water.

NONRENEWABLE RESOURCES

Fossil fuels are naturally formed inside Earth over time. The fossil fuels we use today formed millions of years ago. The process begins with sunlight. The sun's energy helps plants grow. Animals eat these plants. When plants and animals die, their remains break down. Over time, they're buried deep underground and reform as fossil fuels.

Coal forms from plants that once grew on land. Oil and natural gas come from tiny plants and animals that lived in oceans. Fossil fuels are a nonrenewable **resource**, meaning that once they're used, they're gone.

Many people are worried that we're using up our supply of fossil fuels. They also worry about the effect fossil fuels can have on the **environment**. The people in this image are protesting, or speaking out against, the use of fossil fuels.

GETTING HOTTER

Burning fossil fuels produces greenhouse gases. These gases trap heat close to Earth's surface, causing Earth's **temperatures** to rise. This process is called global warming. Global warming changes **habitats** around the world. Deserts become hotter and even the snowy North Pole gets warmer.

The average global temperature has risen 1.4 degrees since 1880. As **glaciers** and other ice formations melt, sea levels rise. Animals that live in cold **climates** lose their homes. Burning fossil fuels for energy is one of the biggest causes of global warming.

CONSERVATION CLUES

Carbon dioxide is a greenhouse gas produced by burning fossil fuels. Human activity has increased the amount of carbon dioxide in the atmosphere by a third.

Energy production from fossil fuels pollutes our air, water, and land. Pollution hurts all living things.

CONSERVATION IS KEY

We need to use fossil fuels more wisely. Conserving energy is an important practice you can start right away. Conserving means limiting how much you use something.

Turn off the lights when you leave a room. Instead of riding in a car, walk or ride your bike when you're going somewhere close by. If you're going a long way, see if it's possible to take a train or bus. Take shorter showers to save water. Small changes in your everyday life can make a big difference!

CONSERVATION CLUES

Recycling is a good way to save energy. It takes less energy to make a product from recycled goods than it does to make something new.

Reading a book, going for a walk, and playing outside are activities that use very little energy. They're fun, too!

SAVING ENERGY WITH THE SUN

Scientists are searching for ways to save energy by using renewable resources. These are natural energy sources such as the sun, wind, and water. Using renewable energy cuts down on the use of fossil fuels.

People collect solar energy with solar panels. These panels turn the sun's energy into electricity for houses and businesses. The sun gives off energy in the form of heat and light. Solar energy can be used to power cars, boats, and spaceships, too.

CONSERVATION CLUES

The International Space Station uses solar panels to create power.

People have been using energy from the sun for thousands of years. When you dry something outside on a hot day, you're using solar energy.

POWERFUL WIND ENERGY

People have learned how to use the power of wind. Early explorers caught the wind in their ships' sails to travel across the seas. Windmills were used to pump water and grind grain. Today, we use wind energy to create electricity.

Wind turbines are very tall objects that often stand in fields. First, wind turns the large blades on top of the tower. The moving blades spin a small rod inside the long pole that holds the turbine. The energy travels to a generator, which makes electricity.

CONSERVATION CLUES

Using wind turbines instead of nonrenewable resources reduces carbon dioxide **emissions**. Right now only about 4 percent of the electricity in the United States is produced by wind energy.

There are about 48,500 wind turbines spread across the United States and Puerto Rico.

WATER WORKS

People need water to fuel their bodies. We also use water to create electricity. This is called hydroelectric power. It's produced when moving water turns a turbine that's joined to a generator. The generator creates electricity.

Hydroelectric plants use dams, which are walls built to control the flow of water. Dams are often built across rivers. The water backed up behind a dam is called a reservoir. Some reservoirs also provide places for people to swim, boat, and have fun.

CONSERVATION CLUES

The generators at the Hoover Dam provide power to the city of Los Angeles, California, and many other locations.

The Hoover Dam has 17 generators. Each generator can supply electricity to 100,000 households.

SPLITTING APART

Everything in the world is made of tiny particles called atoms. Large amounts of energy are stored inside atoms. When atoms are broken apart, the energy inside comes out as heat. The energy made by breaking apart atoms is called nuclear energy.

The heat generated by nuclear power plants is used to boil water and make steam. This steam is used to turn turbines, which creates electricity. However, nuclear power plants produce harmful waste. It must be stored carefully and far away from people.

CONSERVATION CLUES

Geothermal energy is a form of energy that uses heat from beneath Earth's surface to produce electricity.

Nuclear energy produces radioactive waste, which is extremely dangerous. In 1986 the Chernobyl Nuclear Power Plant in Pripyat, Ukraine, exploded. Hundreds of people died and were sickened by the waste from the plant.

MAKING A DIFFERENCE

We use energy in our everyday lives, but eventually our energy sources may run out. It's up to us to find sources of energy that don't harm the environment. Scientists have discovered how to use sunlight, wind, and water to produce energy we can use. A wave power plant off Portugal's coast turns energy from waves into electricity. What could be next?

Make sure to conserve energy when you can. Small actions can make a big difference in protecting Earth's resources.

GLOSSARY

climate: The average weather conditions in an area over a period of time.

destructive: Causing harm or ruin.

emission: Something given off by a source, such as the greenhouse gases given off by a car.

energy crisis: When the demand for energy is greater than what can be supplied by an energy source.

environment: The natural world.

fossil fuels: A fuel—such as coal, oil, or natural gas—that is formed in the earth from dead plants or animals.

glacier: A large mass of ice that moves down a mountain or along a valley.

habitat: The natural home for plants, animals, and other living things.

resource: Something that can be used.

temperature: How hot or cold something is.

INDEX

B
batteries, 4, 5

C
carbon dioxide, 10, 16
cars, 6, 12, 14
Chernobyl, 21
coal, 5, 6, 7, 8

D
dam, 18, 19

E
electricity, 6, 14, 16, 18, 19,
        20, 22

F
fossil fuels, 4, 6, 7, 8, 9, 10,
        11, 12, 14

G
gasoline, 6
generator, 16, 18, 19
geothermal energy, 20
glaciers, 10
global warming, 10
greenhouse gases, 10

H
Hoover Dam, 18, 19
hydroelectric (water) power, 18

I
International Space Station, 14

L
Los Angeles, 18

M
mining, 7

N
natural gas, 6, 7, 8
North Pole, 10
nuclear energy, 20, 21

O
oil, 6, 7, 8

P
pollution, 11
Portugal, 22
power plants, 6, 20, 21, 22

R
radioactive waste, 21
recycling, 12
renewable resources, 14
reservoir, 18

S
solar energy, 14, 15
solar panels, 14

T
turbines, 16, 17, 18, 20

U
United States, 4, 6, 16

W
wind energy, 14, 16, 17
windmills, 16

WEBSITES

Due to the changing nature of Internet links, PowerKids Press has developed an online list of websites related to the subject of this book. This site is updated regularly. Please use this link to access the list: www.powerkidslinks.com/glob/solving